Original title:
Gingerbread Houses and Glowing Fires

Copyright © 2024 Creative Arts Management OÜ
All rights reserved.

Author: Elias Marchant
ISBN HARDBACK: 978-9916-90-942-3
ISBN PAPERBACK: 978-9916-90-943-0

Fireside Magic and Treats

Sitting by the fire, what a sight,
A s'more in hand, oh what a bite!
The marshmallows dance, a gooey show,
While my hair catches fire, oh no, no, no!

The logs crackle while my dog sneezes,
Stirring up smoke like it's winter breezes.
I toss him a biscuit; he looks so refined,
Then snatches my sweater! Oh, good luck I find.

The hot cocoa bubbles, a chocolate dream,
Whipped cream mustache—a sweet little scheme.
I sip and spill, it splatters my nose,
Now my face is a canvas, I've got the prose!

As the shadows dance, tales start to fly,
About a squirrel who thought he could fly.
With a leap and a bound, straight up to a tree,
He realized too late it was a big 'whoopsie'!

So gather 'round friends, let laughter ignite,
With cookies, hot cocoa, and silly delight.
For fireside magic, it's truly a feast,
And the fun only grows, like the marshmallow beast!

A Melting Winter Wonderland

Snowmen melting in the sun,
With carrot noses on the run.
They slide on ice, forget to freeze,
And laugh at children in the sneeze.

Hot cocoa's now a liquid stream,
Where marshmallows used to dream.
Icicles drip like sneaky thieves,
As winter waves its sappy leaves.

Whimsical Dreams by Firelight

Silly shadows dance on walls,
As marshmallows do cartwheels and falls.
The crackling flames tell jolly tales,
Of mischievous gnomes in fuzzy sails.

Warm socks wiggle, they can't be still,
While sleepy eyes begin to chill.
A dream of cookies and milk does rise,
As ice cream floats in the night skies.

Emberlit Secrets of Sweetness

The cookies giggle in the bowl,
As sugar sprinkles take a stroll.
Cinnamon sticks hold hands in glee,
While chocolate chips play hide and see.

Frosting rivers flow so thick,
While candy canes do a little trick.
Whipped cream clouds float by the way,
And lollipop rainbows make the day.

A Flurry of Frosted Delights

Sprinkles tumble, dizzy in flight,
While cupcakes boast of their sweet bite.
Frosty cookies are wearing hats,
Twirling in dance with the hungry cats.

Gumdrops giggle in a candy spree,
As licorice vines climb up a tree.
The gingerbread men are on the run,
Chasing after the gingerbread fun.

Glimmering Edibility

In the fridge, a treat does gleam,
A jello wiggle, a sugary dream.
Carrots laugh, they're not on the list,
Next to the cake, they feel quite missed.

A chocolate fountain, the grandest sight,
Dunking marshmallows, oh, what a plight!
The cookies whisper, 'You're losing the fight!'
Crumbs on my shirt, a sweet dinner blight.

Gummy bears dance with such flair,
On a licorice rug, without a care.
With gummy worms wriggling around,
It's a candy party, joy unbound.

So bring on the sweets, let the giggles flow,
For in this kitchen, there's always a show.
With sugar and laughter, we'll conquer the night,
For glimmering edibility brings pure delight!

Enchanted Candied Refuge

In a forest where lollipops grow,
Peppermints sprout in a candy-filled show.
Chocolate rivers flow all around,
In this enchanted refuge, joy's always found.

Gumdrops glisten like stars up high,
Soda pop rain falls from the sky.
The marshmallow trees sway without fright,
Under the moonlight, they glow so bright.

With jellybeans as comfy chairs,
And licorice paths leading to lairs,
Every gummy critter sings and prances,
In this sugary haven, everyone dances.

So gather your friends, let's frolic and play,
In this candyland realm, we'll eat all day.
For in enchanted candied refuge so sweet,
Our laughter and joy will never face defeat!

A Warm Embrace in Sugar

A cupcake hugs you with frosting so nice,
Sprinkles sprinkle love, it's a sugar paradise.
In a cookie's embrace, the crunch feels just right,
As we nibble together, our smiles are bright.

Chocolate chips wink from a gooey delight,
In brownies so fudgy, they put up a fight.
Whipped cream whispers, 'I'm just here for fun!'
In this sweet hug, we're never done.

Gingerbread hugs coming in hot,
With icing smiles, they give it a shot.
In this warm embrace of sugar and cheer,
We feast till our tummies can no longer steer.

So let's raise a toast with this syrupy cheer,
In this sugary haven, there's nothing to fear.
With laughter and love, let's fill every plate,
For a warm embrace in sugar is truly first rate!

The Lure of Luminescence

Under the stars, cookies glow bright,
Twinkling like gems on a romantic night.
Sugar beams dance on the plate with glee,
Inviting us in, it's a sight to see.

Marshmallow moons float high overhead,
While gummy stars twinkle, their sweetness widespread.
We gather around, sharing laughter and dreams,
In a world where sugar glows and beams.

The lure of luminescence calls us near,
As we feast on candy, releasing all fear.
Crackers snap while jelly beans cheer,
In this bright wonderland, nothing is drear.

So come take a bite of the radiant sights,
In a candy cosmos, where joy ignites.
For in this sweet realm, happiness thrives,
With luminescent treats, our laughter survives!

Sweet Sanctuary

In a world where sugar rain,
Gummy bears dance down the lane.
Chocolate rivers flow with glee,
Welcome to my candy spree!

Candy canes in high supply,
Marshmallows bounce, they never lie.
Lollipops twirl with great delight,
In this land, snacks take flight!

Cupcakes sing a sugary tune,
As fudge clouds float beneath the moon.
Jelly beans jump and cheer,
In my sweet sanctuary, never fear!

So grab a treat, let worries go,
In this haven of snack-filled glow.
With every bite, joy takes its part,
Sweet sanctuary, a sugary heart!

The Lively Light of Sweets

Underneath a candy moon,
Chocolate dreams come all too soon.
Gumdrops shine like stars at night,
In this place, all feels just right.

Licorice paths that twist and crawl,
Jelly beans bounce and have a ball.
Every lick of ice cream brings,
Joy that only summer flings.

Sprinkle fairies flutter by,
Turning donuts into pie.
Cotton candy clouds up high,
In this world, we reach for the sky!

A giggle here, a chuckle there,
Every nibble without a care.
In the lively light so sweet,
Life is just a tasty treat!

Candy House Whisperings

Whispers in the candy air,
Gingersnaps fill every chair.
Chocolate doors creak open wide,
Let the scrumptious times abide!

Marzipan and sugar high,
Lemon drops that make you sigh.
Cupcake rain on frosting floor,
Candy house, we want some more!

Twizzlers hanging from the beams,
S'mores muffins are our dreams.
Every corner holds a tale,
Of sweet mischief, never stale!

In the cupboard, sweets conspire,
Giggling softly, lifting higher.
Through the laughter, secrets flow,
Candy house, where dreams do glow!

Embraced by Warmth

In a world of gooey bliss,
Fudgy hugs that you can't miss.
Caramel rivers, soft and wide,
Embraced by warmth, let joy abide!

Candy apples shine so bright,
Cinnamon rolls, a sweet delight.
Every morsel sings a song,
In this haven, we belong.

Marshmallow cushions, soft as air,
Chocolate hugs, beyond compare.
Sweet embrace of every treat,
In this warmth, life feels complete!

So snuggle close in cookie cheer,
Every bite brings laughter near.
Embraced by warmth, let's celebrate,
In this sweet world, it's never late!

The Making of Magic in the Dark

In shadows deep where wizards lurk,
I tripped on a wand, oh what a quirk!
Brewed potions in my mom's old sock,
Turned my pet cat into a rock.

I sprinkled some spice, not meant for sweets,
Now every mouse makes the strangest tweets.
With wands and spells like a topsy-turvy kite,
I conjured a goblin to fix my light.

Sweets Beyond the Hearth

The gingerbread men have taken a stand,
Demanding more sugar, oh isn't that grand?
Frosting rivers flowed down my chair,
A candy cane army marched without a care.

Chocolate spills like laughter and cheer,
The marshmallows giggle when I draw near.
I offered them cookies, they turned me away,
Said they'd rather have cupcakes for breakfast today.

Flickering Joys in Candied Corners

In the candy shop where confetti spills,
Gummy bears gossip, giving me thrills.
Chocolate fountains erupt in delight,
While lollipops twirl, an outrageous sight.

The jellybeans jump; they love to dance,
Each color a tune, oh what a chance!
Licorice ropes become playful snakes,
Winding around all my sweet lil' mistakes.

Twinkling Embers and Baked Memories

In the oven where dreams bake bright,
I once left my socks—what a fright!
The cookies sang as they turned crusty,
A dance of flour, both bold and rusty.

The pie tried to run, but got stuck in the pan,
Desserts have ambitions, oh yes, they can!
As I spooned on the filling, it plopped like a dream,
Twinkling embers whispered, "This is our theme!"

The Comfort of Toffee

Toffee so sweet, a warm delight,
Soft caramel hugs, in each bite.
It whispers sweet secrets, oh so strong,
In a world of sugar, where we belong.

Chews of happiness, they make you smile,
Stuck to your teeth for a little while.
A comforting crunch, a cozy glow,
Who needs therapy when you've got toffee flow?

Chocolate rivers, flowing with glee,
Toffee boats sailing, just you and me.
Sugar-coated dreams, what a hoot,
Toffee is therapy in dessert suit!

So grab a piece, don't you delay,
Life's little pleasures are here to stay.
In the comfort of toffee, we all converge,
A sweet little world where joy can emerge.

Warm Colors and Candy Lines

Warm colors swirl, like a sunset bright,
Marshmallows dance in the soft twilight.
With candy lines drawn, we paint the sky,
Let's eat our way up, reaching so high.

Lollipops twirl in a rainbow arc,
Fizzy colors that leave a mark.
A burst of laughter, a sugary tease,
Life is a canvas, oh such a breeze!

Syrupy swirls that make us grin,
With every bite, we're ready to spin.
In this sweet palette, we find our muse,
Candy-coated joys, you just can't refuse!

So take my hand, let's stroll along,
In this candy dream, everything's strong.
With warm colors bright, life's just divine,
Let's savor the sweetness, in candy lines!

Flickers of the Past

Nostalgic snacks that used to be,
Bubblicious gum and Tootsie free.
Flickers of laughter from years gone by,
With candy memories, we never say die.

Candy corn dreams of Halloween night,
When treats were plenty, and all felt right.
In a landslide of sugar, we'd live it up,
Dipping our spoons in the sweet syrup cup.

Popping up memories like popcorn balls,
Sharing our stories in the sweet stalls.
With every bite, a tale comes alive,
In the whirl of the past, our spirits thrive.

So let's raise a toast with gummy bears,
To those flickers of joy, and sweet affairs.
In candy-coated worlds, we find our zest,
Reliving our youth, oh isn't it the best?

Enchantment in Every Bite

Chocolate castles and candy lands,
Enchanting flavors in our hands.
With every bite, magic unfolds,
Sweet stories told in bits of gold.

Gummies that giggle and chocolates that sing,
Candy canes dancing with every spring.
A sprinkle of laughter, a dash of cheer,
In enchanted bites, joy's always near.

Soda pop fizz with a burst of delight,
Each sip a spell, twinkling so bright.
In this sugary realm, we're lost in the fun,
Chasing sweet dreams 'til the day is done.

So savor the magic with every treat,
In this world of wonder, life's truly sweet.
For in every bite, we find our might,
Enchanted by candy, hearts take flight!

Hearthside Memories in Molasses

In a kitchen where cookies get stuck,
We search for a spatula, oh what luck!
Molasses drips down like a slow-motion race,
Mom's face turns to horror, it's a sticky embrace.

Grandpa sits back with a grin and a chuckle,
Spills of brown sugar start giving him trouble.
"Just lick your fingers, it's all in good fun!"
But the cat now looks like he's just on the run.

A burst of laughter fills up the abode,
While we sweep crumbs from the overly-bowed.
"Next time let's bake while we're just in our sweats,"
And dream of the sweets we might undermine yet.

With memories toasted like marshmallows warm,
We sip cocoa from mugs, in the holiday storm.
So here's to the mess that we always adore,
For laughter in chaos, we couldn't ask more!

Enchanted Structures of Delight

In a land where pop-tarts grow as tall as a tree,
And chocolate rivers flow wild and free,
We fashioned a castle of cookies and sprinkles,
But the walls, oh dear, let out giggles and crinkles.

A moat made of milk with a bridge of gummy bears,
Guards with licorice swords, with licorice flares,
The drawbridge is made from sheets of fine taffy,
But be careful, my friend; it's a tad too sappy!

Baking disasters were memos from fate,
But we built a domain that no one could hate.
With frosting confetti to crown every spire,
Our town may be sweet, but we dare not aspire!

In this sugary realm, whimsies take flight,
Where every day's filled with a chuckle or bite.
So join in the fun, don't bother to pout,
For structures of delight are what it's about!

Ember-Kissed Windows

From the snug little cabana with candles aglow,
We peek through the windows, watching the snow,
With noses all red and cups filled with cheer,
Stories of mischief tickle the ear.

A snowman once danced, or should we say swayed?
With a carrot for a nose, he looked quite afraid.
But laughter erupted as he lost his top hat,
And rolled with the snow, how silly is that?

Outside the frost bitten trees, all agleam,
Inside we're unsure if it's night or daydream.
The warmth of the hearth sings joy with a tune,
While we swap our old tales under the cold moon.

So here's to the windows that frame winter nights,
Where laughter and warmth ignite our delights.
Ember-kissed moments where smiles shine bright,
We cozy together till first morning light!

Sweet Shadows on a Winter's Eve

As shadows stretch long across frosty ground,
With blankets of snow, the stillness resounds,
We sit by the fire, a marshmallow's fate,
Toasting and roasting, it's never too late.

The cat pounces gently, disguised as a round,
He thinks he's a hero—oh what a profound!
Flopping on laps, he claims royal decree,
While giggles erupt like a spill from a spree.

Outside, icicles dangle, like fangs from a beast,
But inside it's warmth, fun, and laughter—at least,
With cookies all crumbling and tea steeped so slow,
We cling to the sweetness, we nibble, we glow.

So here's to the shadows on this winter's night,
Where the quirks of the season bring joy and delight.
May the laughter rebound like a spare on repeat,
And stay sweet like the treats we forever repeat!

Frosted Fantasy and Fiery Embrace

In winter's breath, the cookies glow,
With icing rivers, all in a row.
But when I bite, oh what a tease,
It's all just crumbs, like stolen cheese.

The elves are busy, baking pies,
In tiny boots, they dance and fly.
But when they trip, and faceplant down,
The flour flies, they look like clowns.

A snowman asks for extra cream,
While sipping cocoa like a dream.
His carrot nose, a bent old straw,
Awake the neighbors with his snore!

So when you see the frosted treats,
Remember, first, it's fun to greet.
For joy is found in every bite,
Just watch your waist, or hold on tight!

Sugar Crystals in the Hearthlight

A candy cane sat on my desk,
I thought, 'Oh what a sweet request!'
But when I tried to have a taste,
It turned to mush, what a disgrace!

The gingerbread house built with care,
Now welcomes ants to have a share.
They munch the roof and chew the door,
My sweet abode now's a bug's store.

Hot chocolate spills on my warm lap,
I lose my phone in the chocolate trap.
With whipped cream hat and marshmallow boots,
I'm serving snacks, but look like fruits!

So next time you bake a festive loaf,
Be warned, my friend, it's not a trope.
For sugar can bring more than cheer,
A sticky mess is always near!

Luminous Dreams of Spice and Sugar

The spice jar danced beneath the light,
Cinnamon twirled with pure delight.
Nutmeg joined in with a wink and a grin,
Spices mixing like a joyful din.

A pie in the oven starts to sing,
The melody of winter brings.
But wait, what's that? Oh, burnt, oh no!
My dreams of dessert, now ashes in tow!

With sugar plums that dance and prance,
I stumbled upon their merry dance.
But when they saw me, they kicked up high,
And straight in my face, they made me cry!

Sugary dreams quickly turn to froth,
As I fall asleep in a scone-baked cloth.
So if you're baking, heed my tale,
Beware the whims of the sugar trail!

Tinsel-Topped Warmth

The tinsel sparkles on the tree,
But dangled low, it caught my knee.
A cat emerged all full of cheer,
And wrapped himself with holiday fear.

The lights above began to flicker,
I thought they'd go out, then go quicker.
But with a laugh and some cheer,
They just got tangled, without any fear.

My aunt brought cookies, stacked so high,
But before we ate, one flew by!
A little kid lunged for the prize,
And mom just sighed, with rolling eyes.

So as we gather around the glow,
With laughter shared, and voices low.
Let's toast to messes, joy in the fray,
In this tinsel-topped, warm holiday!

Cocoa-coated Corners

In a corner so sweet, with cocoa galore,
I found chocolate bunnies, oh what a score!
They winked at me sly, with a grin on their face,
I left out some cookies, they quickened their pace.

Marshmallow fluff clouds drifted down from above,
While the candy cane trees whispered love.
Gumdrops like raindrops fell soft on the ground,
A world made of sweets, where joy could be found.

The walls were all draped with licorice lace,
I danced with the cupcakes, a sweet sugar race.
Chocolate rivers flowed, oh what a delight,
In this cocoa-coated haven, everything's right.

But watch out, here comes a giraffe with a hat,
Serving hot cocoa while juggling a cat!
In this corner of sweets, we laugh till we drop,
With chocolate delights, we'll never ever stop!

Winter's Fiery Embrace

Winter arrived with a blanket so white,
But deep in my heart, it was cozy and bright.
With mittens and hats, I ventured outside,
But slipped on some ice, oh what a wild ride!

Snowflakes like confetti danced in the air,
As snowmen were built with a whimsical flair.
They sported a scarf, with a grin carved wide,
But one took a tumble, oh, how we all cried!

Hot cocoa was brewing, marshmallows afloat,
Sipping it slowly, in my warm winter coat.
But the cat jumped right in, oh dear, what a mess,
Now he's a cocoa-coat kitty, I must confess!

With snowball fights breaking out all around,
The laughter erupted, the joy was profound.
In winter's embrace, with the fire burning bright,
We'll cherish these moments, all through the night!

Sweetscape Symphony

A symphony played with the sweetest of treats,
Where chocolate and jellybeans dance on the beats.
The gummy bears groove, with a rhythm so sweet,
While the licorice violins play candy cane beats.

Fudge flows like water in this magical place,
Where jelly rolls tumble with sugar and grace.
The marshmallow trumpets announce every cue,
As the lollipop dancers twirl, oh so true!

The fruit gummies sang in a fruity delight,
While caramel drizzles twinkled in the night.
The cotton candy clouds floated high in the air,
For a sweetscape symphony, beyond compare!

As I savored each note of this sugary score,
I knew I could always return for more.
With every sweet treat, my heart danced in tune,
In this candy-coated concert, under the moon!

Cozy Creations

In a cozy little nook, with a blanket so warm,
Sat a cat with a hat, in all of her charm.
She knitted some socks, her paws working fast,
But she tangled them up! Those stitches didn't last.

A teapot was whistling, inviting and sweet,
With biscuits and scones, oh what a great treat!
But the dog stole a biscuit, oh what a surprise,
Now they're both chasing crumbs, with mischief in their eyes!

The fireplace crackled, with flames doing a dance,
While ghosts made of yarn took the chance to prance.
They tangled my slippers, oh what a sight,
In this cozy creation, the laughter feels right!

So here in this chaos, with joy all around,
In a home full of giggles, happiness found.
With coffee and mischief, and pets by my side,
In this cozy creation, I'll happily bide!

The Glow of Sweets

In a kitchen where sugar finds its glow,
Marshmallows waltz, putting on a show.
Chocolates giggle, oh what a sight,
Candies throw confetti, celebrating the night.

Gumdrops roll in their colorful spree,
Lollipops swirl, they're dancing with glee.
Frosting fights with sprinkles in a bowl,
Cookies team up to conquer their role.

Syrups are sticky, they claim the throne,
While cupcakes squabble, they're never alone.
Let's raise a toast with a fizzy pop cheer,
To the glow of sweets that brings us such gear.

Hearthfire Hues

In the kitchen, warmth spreads through the air,
Potatoes begin their fluffy affair.
Carrots wear jackets of butter and gold,
Bristling with laughter, every dish bold.

The oven hums a delightful song,
While little herbs dance all the day long.
Garlic and onions join in the fun,
While spices cheer, 'We've just begun!'

Pies bubble over, they're feeling so grand,
With crusts that are flaky, aren't they just planned?
Hearthfire hues warm every cold night,
Creating dishes that taste just right!

Sugar and Solace

When life gets tough, grab a sugary treat,
Chocolate or gummy, oh what a feat!
Fudge forms a bridge to a happier place,
With ice cream floods, let worries erase.

Cake crumbs flutter like butterflies bright,
Pies twinkle like stars on a cozy night.
Hold tight to marshmallows, soft as a breeze,
For they're sugar hugs, guaranteed to please.

Cookies come marching, a parade of delight,
While cupcakes frolic in frosting's delight.
Sugar and solace, they're the perfect pair,
Life's little sweetness, beyond compare.

Twinkling Confections

Twinkling confections, all sprinkled with glee,
Dancing on plates like they're at a jubilee.
Fizzy lollipops with laughter in-show,
Baking up giggles wherever they go.

Candy canes strut like they own the street,
While jelly beans pop to the funky beat.
In this sweet circus, how could we frown?
Dessert's our jester, wearing a crown!

Chocolate rivers flowing like joyful streams,
Cotton candy clouds fill our sweetest dreams.
In this world of treats, we find our bliss,
Twinkling confections, oh, what a sweet kiss!

Cozy Corners

In the corner where the cat lays,
He dreams of tuna-filled days.
A sock on the floor, a cup of tea,
This cluttered paradise is blissful glee.

Grandma's chair, its fabric worn,
She swears it's where the best jokes are born.
With every creak and every bounce,
Her tales make us laugh, they truly renounce.

Mismatched cushions in a pile,
Each one has a unique, goofy style.
They hold the secrets of all our friends,
And giggles echo, the joy never ends.

Little plants with faces painted,
Staring at us, slightly tainted.
They probably think we're quite absurd,
But they still listen to every word.

Flickers of Fondness

In the kitchen, cookies burn bright,
Sweet smells turn to a smoke-filled fright.
Recipes that seem so divine,
Turn into laughs, and that's just fine.

Old photo albums tossed on the floor,
Grandpa's hair was once a lion's roar.
We giggle at outfits from years gone by,
& wonder how did we think they were fly?

Mom's attempts at cool dance moves,
More like a chicken, but she sure grooves.
We mimic her style with silly grace,
And video record for posterity's case.

Shared stories in the glow of the light,
As flickering candles dance in the night.
These moments of laughter, joy intertwined,
In the flickers of fondness, love we will find.

Heartwarming Hearths

The fireplace crackles with a pop,
Marshmallows flying, we can't make them stop.
S'mores turn into a gooey affair,
Chocolate faces, sugary hair.

Family debates on the best game to play,
"Uno!" "Monopoly!" shouts little Jay.
While Grandpa snores in his comfy chair,
We'll just add more snacks; he won't even care.

Giggles and stories start to unfold,
About the wild times when we were bold.
Candles flicker, the room fills with cheer,
Heartwarming hearths bring everyone near.

As the night deepens, we share our dreams,
Laughter echoes, or so it seems.
Wrapped up tight in a blanket of love,
These moments are blessings sent from above.

Tasty Temptations

Pizza toppings that dance on the crust,
Pineapple's welcome, it's a must!
But Aunt Sue claims it's a culinary crime,
Arguments abound over slices and time.

Baking cupcakes, what a delight,
Frosting fights that are quite the sight.
Sprinkles fly like confetti in air,
And laughter erupts without a care.

Chili so spicy, it tingles your nose,
One little bite, and everyone knows.
We gasp and laugh, reach for the milk,
"Take a sip, it's just like silk!"

Around the table, stories we share,
About food adventures and kitchen despair.
Tasty temptations, a feast for the soul,
These moments together make our hearts whole.

Warm Thymes and Cinnamon Nights

On chilly eves, the stew does bubble,
With thyme and spice, who needs the trouble?
A sneeze erupts, oh what a sight,
My dinner's flying — dinner takes flight!

The cookies dance and sway with glee,
Choco chips calling, "Come, snack with me!"
I dip my toes in pots so hearty,
This warm thyme stew? It's quite the party!

A dash of salt, a twist of fate,
I burn my toast — oh, what a plate!
But laughter fills the kitchen bright,
With cinnamon nights and pure delight!

So if you stumble, trip, or fall,
Just sprinkle sugar, and hear the call.
For every mess, there's joy in sight,
In warm thymes and cinnamon nights!

A Hearth of Golden Sweets

In a cozy nook, where pastries rise,
Golden sweets dance before our eyes.
The pie sings songs of buttery glaze,
Its warm embrace, a sugary haze.

Beneath the lamp, the cookies gleam,
Frosting drips like a dentist's dream.
The chocolate flows, a river wide,
In this sweet hearth, we take our pride.

When cake collapses, and bread is tough,
I grin and nod, "This is just enough!"
A sprinkle here, a frosting swish,
We still have fun, that's our main dish!

So gather 'round this delight so neat,
With every treat, our hearts will meet.
In a hearth of golden sweets, we greet,
Laughter and joy make life complete!

The Edible Abode Beneath the Stars

In a house of candy, beneath the night,
Gummy bears laugh; oh, what a sight!
Chocolate doors swing open wide,
Marshmallow walls, come on inside!

The roof's made of cookies, fresh and warm,
A gummy bear guard, that's the norm.
An avalanche of sprinkles, rain down,
In this edible dream, I'm the crowned clown!

But beware the sugar monster's wrath,
It lurks and waits, hiding its path.
Stepping lightly, I sneak a treat,
A licorice vine, oh so sweet!

So gaze above at the sugary stars,
In this abode, we'll raise our jars.
To the edible night and all its charms,
With laughter and joy, we'll fill our arms!

Luminous Lairs of Spice

In the kitchen's glow, spices ignite,
Ginger and clove dance under the light.
A splash of nutmeg, a wink of thyme,
Cooking up jokes, oh isn't it prime?

The pots start to bubble, the pans all sing,
Food is the joy that laughter will bring.
As garlic wafts like a spell in the air,
"Who turned that on?" I glance everywhere!

With every stir, a story unfolds,
Of tamales made and chili that holds.
So let's toss a pinch and twirl with grace,
In these luminous lairs, spice finds its place!

So grab a fork, and join in the cheer,
For laughter and flavor, we'll always adhere.
In kitchens bright with memories and mirth,
Let's feast and celebrate this lovely earth!

Radiant Restoration

In the morning, I found my sock,
It was hiding behind the clock.
Radiant rays from my coffee cup,
Woke me gently, 'Time to sup.'

The dog snored loud, a timbered beast,
Dreaming of treats, his greatest feast.
I tiptoed slow, careful not to wake,
My breakfast dreams were mine to make.

A spoon flew high, a cereal kite,
Sailing through space, what a funny sight!
Landed in milk with a splash, oh dear,
Breakfast's chaos, best time of year.

With laughter loud, we clean the mess,
Every spilled flake becomes a bless.
Together we smile, then pout, then grin,
Oh, breakfast joys, let the day begin!

Cottage of Cravings

In a cottage built of sweet delight,
Cookies and cakes dance in the light.
Brownies whisper secrets they keep,
While the ice cream sings me to sleep.

Pies lay waiting, all warm and round,
Each slice a treasure, a delight found.
I took a bite and heard a squeal:
'It's magic here – you know the deal!'

Chocolate rivers flowed by the door,
Marshmallow clouds made us want more.
Gummy bears bounced on jelly floors,
In this cottage, we can't keep scores.

Together we feast, it's a candy spree,
A buffet of dreams, all sugary glee.
In our cozy nook, we laugh and we play,
In a cottage of cravings, we'll never stray!

Warmth Wrapped in Sugar

Wrapped up tight like a cocoon,
I found my sweets, oh, what a boon!
Sugar hugs and marshmallow cheer,
In this warmth, I've naught to fear.

The cookies wink, their frosting gleams,
While candy canes float in my dreams.
A chocolate blanket covers all,
In this sweet world, I stand tall.

Cupcakes smile with sprinkles bright,
Macarons giggle in sheer delight.
Together we dance, our hearts in sync,
In the warmth of sugar, we seldom think.

Sitting back, we let out a sigh,
With a sugary treat, we touch the sky.
Wrapped in sweetness, our troubles flee,
In this cozy haven, just you and me!

The Spice of Togetherness

In the kitchen, a sprinkle of fun,
Gather 'round, everyone, here we come!
The spice is lively, dancing around,
Seasoned laughter is the best sound.

Garlic giggles and onion sighs,
Every chopped veggie, a tasty surprise.
With a stir and a dash, we blend our hearts,
In this lovely dish, togetherness starts.

Taco night brings all flavors bold,
We pile our plates, no one's controlled.
Cheese piling higher, won't let it drop,
In the spice of share, we'll never stop.

Holding hands, we watch the pot boil,
Sharing our stories with love and toil.
In this warm kitchen, life's a sweet test,
With the spice of togetherness, we are blessed!

Cozy Retreats of Flour

In a kitchen corner, dough does lie,
With flour clouds that reach the sky.
Cookies whisper, sweetly tease,
While I strategize to grab some cheese.

A rolling pin, my trusty sidekick,
We flatten worries with every flick.
A sprinkle here, a drizzle there,
The perfect bread, beyond compare!

The oven hums a cozy tune,
Who knew baking could be a boon?
As bread rises, so does my cheer,
Next stop: pastry, bring it near!

So grab a seat, don't be a bore,
Join me here for cravings galore.
In this retreat of joy and fun,
Let's bake and laugh until we're done!

Twinkling Tastes

A chocolate cake in the making,
Oh, the secrets it's faking!
A pinch of sugar, a splash of glee,
Time to taste—who's bold as me?

Sprinkles jump in a rainbow dance,
While I ponder this baking chance.
Lemon zest with a zingy grin,
Twinkling tastes, let the feast begin!

Ice cream winks from the freezer's door,
"Take me, I'm ready for more!"
Drizzled syrup on top like a crown,
Messy faces in this sweet town!

Even broccoli wants to be fried,
But tonight, it's desserts we'll ride.
Taste buds twinkle, join the cheer,
The sweetest moments, oh-so-clear!

Embers and Edibles

The campfire crackles with tasty flair,
Marshmallows toast in the cool night air.
Chocolate dripping, graham crackin',
S'mores so gooey, ain't no lackin'!

Hot dogs sizzle with a juicy song,
If only I'd packed a skillet along.
Beans in a can, a culinary test,
Competing for dinner, they're far from the best!

Yet laughter crackles like the flame,
As we joke, and it's never the same.
We share ghost stories, with snacks in hand,
In this ember glow, we all make a stand!

So gather 'round, let your voices soar,
With embers and edibles, we'll always want more.
In the fire's warmth, we'll dream and toast,
For sweet campfire nights, we shall boast!

Bright Spirits Among Pastries

Bakeries buzzing with life and cheer,
Croissants whisper, 'Come and steer!'
Bright spirits roll in like a doughy wave,
Flaky pastries, oh how they crave!

Cupcakes giggle with frosting crowns,
As donuts dance in playful gowns.
Eclairs waltz on the counter's top,
While brownies hop, 'We'll never stop!'

Flaky pies tell tales of fruit and zest,
Muffins tease with 'who's the best?'
Each morsel smiles, a tasty friend,
In this pastry realm, it'll never end!

So raise a fork, and let's make a toast,
To bright spirits, enjoy what we boast.
In sweet delight, we'll twirl and spin,
Among pastries bright, let the fun begin!

Cozy Candied Corners

In corners sweet, the candies lay,
A chocolate bar just miles away.
Jellybeans bounce, like kids at play,
In this sugary haven, we'll forever stay.

Gummy bears dance on the shelf,
Sipping soda, sharing themselves.
Marshmallow fluff, what a delight,
Turn off the lights, let's party all night!

Licorice ropes tie our fate,
Candy corn whispers, 'Isn't this great?'
Fortified by treats we adore,
Who needs health when you've got sugar galore?

So come to this corner, grab your share,
In cozy delight, we haven't a care.
With sweetened smiles and sugary cheer,
We'll feast till the morrow, oh dear, oh dear!

Welcoming Warmth

The sun peeks in through the window bright,
Inviting us all to bask in its light.
With coffee in hand and a warm, soft chair,
It feels like a hug, with warmth to spare.

Cookies are baking, oh what a scent!
A sprinkle of magic in every event.
The laughter and joy dance in the air,
Sharing warmth, knowing we deeply care.

A quilt on the couch, snug and tight,
Cuddles and stories last through the night.
With memories woven into each seam,
We cradle our dreams in a cozy beam.

So gather around, let us be merry,
With warmth as our guide, we'll never be wary.
Holding hands, hearts intertwined,
In this welcome warmth, pure love we find.

The Sweet Glow of Evening

As day turns to dusk with a sweet, soft sigh,
The fireflies twinkle, lighting up the sky.
A pastel twilight paints the scene,
Where laughter and joy meet the atmosphere serene.

The crickets begin their symphonic show,
Casting a spell as the cool breezes blow.
With ice cream in bowls, toppings galore,
We savor each bite, begging for more!

So let's gather 'round under the moon's soft glow,
Sharing our jokes, making giggles flow.
Like chocolate fountains, our spirits rise,
In the sweet glow of evening, our hearts harmonize.

So here's to the laughter, the stories we weave,
In this magical hour, we truly believe.
We'll carve out our memories with joy that won't end,
In the sweet glow of evening, together with friends.

Spice-scented Stories

In a kitchen filled with a fragrant bliss,
Where cinnamon whispers and spices kiss.
A pot on the stove, bubbling away,
Pulls us together for stories to play.

Nutmeg tales and gingerbread dreams,
We share the laughter, hear the giggles' screams.
While rolling the dough, we twirl and spin,
In this spice-scented world, we all fit in.

Clove and allspice, the scent of delight,
Binds our hearts as we cook through the night.
With every stir, a memory's made,
In this pantry of life, let worries fade.

So come join the fun, let's sprinkle the joy,
With spice-scented stories, no one can annoy.
In our cozy kitchen, with friends so true,
We'll whip up some magic and laughter, too!

Frosted Fantasy Abode

In a house of sugar, I reside,
With frosting dreams where candies glide,
Windows made of chocolate cream,
Silly thoughts, a frosted dream.

Lollipops guard my candy door,
They sway and dance, what's there in store?
Jelly beans in every nook,
An edible, magical storybook.

Cupcake clouds in the bright blue sky,
I take a bite, and oh my, oh my!
Sprinkle rain falls down with glee,
In my sweet home, life's a spree.

Buttercream pillows, jellybean beds,
Gummy bears float in my head,
In this house where wishes come true,
Frosted fun, so much to chew!

Toasted Marshmallow Memories

Toasty tales around the fire,
Marshmallows dancing, never tire,
Sticky fingers, laughter loud,
S'mores and giggles make us proud.

Chocolate rivers, graham cracker shores,
Happiness flows; who could ask for more?
Roasted dreams, they meld and blend,
In this sweet space, joy has no end.

Nighttime whispers, ghostly sights,
A marshmallow moon on starry nights,
Pillow fights with fluff and glee,
Toasty memories, just you and me!

Campfire songs, a serenade,
Melting marshmallows, a sugar parade,
In this chapter, forever we'll stay,
Toasty marshmallow memories, bright and gay!

Sugar Silk Shadows

In a world where sweets softly fall,
Sugar silk shadows beckon to all,
Candy-coated wishes roam free,
Laughter lingers like honeyed tea.

Chocolate rivers and candy trees,
Whispers of sugar float on the breeze,
Twinkling stars made of spiced cake,
In this sweet realm, dreams we bake.

Gummy bears dance in their jelly shoes,
Twirling around with nothing to lose,
Fizzy pop dreams like fireworks soar,
Sugar silk shadows, forevermore!

Listen closely to the laughter near,
Tastes so sweet we hold dear,
In this dessert-like daydream glow,
Sugar silk shadows, the best show!

The Cozy Confection

In a nook made of candy and fluff,
Life's a sweet ride, never too tough,
Gingerbread houses, cozy and bright,
Where dessert adventures take flight.

With licorice whips and nutty delights,
Every heartbeat sings through sugary nights,
Chocolate hugs wrapped all around,
In this cozy confection, joy is found.

Whipped cream clouds, soft as a sigh,
Floating along where all sweets lie,
Every nibble brings giggles anew,
In this cozy place, dreams come true!

Sprinkled whimsies, laughter so sweet,
Join the party, won't take a seat,
In this sugary haven, forever we stay,
Blissful days in the sweetest way!

Sweet Retreats

When chocolate calls, I must obey,
A candy trip, let's laugh and play.
With gummy bears that dance and twirl,
Each bite a sweet, delightful whirl.

Ice cream sundaes, stacked so tall,
A mountain high, oh, please don't fall.
Whipped cream clouds and cherry skies,
In this retreat, all diets die.

Cupcakes frosted, rainbow dreams,
Life's a party, bursting seams.
Syrupy rivers, caramel streams,
In sugary land, we burst at the seams.

So grab a spoon, let's dive right in,
In this sweet world, we always win.
Keep your worries, we'll have a treat,
Join me now, my sugar sweet!

Nostalgia in Confection

Remember the days of bubblegum bliss?
The fizzy soda, oh how could we miss?
With candy necklaces and licorice whips,
Each flavor burst bringing laughter to lips.

Pop rocks crackle, a candy delight,
While marshmallow fluff takes our taste buds flight.
Growing up, our pockets were full,
Of all the sweets that made us pull.

The smell of fresh cookies, warm from the oven,
In grandma's kitchen, sweet memories lovin'.
Chocolate chips and sprinkles galore,
These sugary treasures, we always adore.

Now we reminisce with a smile so wide,
As we savor these treats with every bite.
Nostalgia's sweet, a glorious blend,
In every confection, memories send.

Firelight Reflections

By the campfire, we toast marshmallows,
As shadows dance like chocolate-fueled fellows.
S'mores stacked high, gooey and sweet,
With laughter and stories, our favorite treat.

The crackle of wood, the pop of the flame,
Telling tall tales, games played without shame.
Each sticky finger, each gooey embrace,
Under starry skies, we find our place.

The warmth of the fire, the glow on our face,
Melting chocolate, a sugary grace.
Swapping sweet bites while the night grows old,
In the glow of the fire, sweet tales unfold.

So let's gather 'round, with treats in tow,
With sugary delights, our spirits will grow.
Firelight reflections and marshmallow dreams,
In this sweet moment, nothing's as it seems.

Sugar-Glazed Moments

In a world of sweets, I stumble and fall,
Tripping over donuts, oh what a brawl!
With frosting-filled dreams, I laugh and I cheer,
In a sugar-glazed moment, there's nothing to fear.

The ring of a bagel, a cinnamon swirl,
Life is a pastry, let flavors unfurl!
Each bite is a giggle, a sweet-sparkling laugh,
With pancakes stacked high, let's do the math.

Jelly beans bouncing, a colorful spree,
With rainbow fruit rolls, as chewy as can be!
In this sugary realm, let whispers take flight,
As we dance through the kitchen, pure joy and delight.

So cherish each sugar-glazed, happy feat,
For life is a treat, and oh, what a sweet!
With laughter and smiles, we savor the fun,
In sugary moments, there's never just one.

Hearth and Home

In the kitchen, pots collide,
With a dance of spices, side by side.
The cat's on the counter, what a sight,
Stealing fish, oh, a culinary fright!

The oven hums a merry tune,
As flour flutters like a cartoon.
Mom shouts, 'Don't wear that dough!'
But sticky fingers steal the show!

Grandpa snoozes in his chair,
With drool that could fill a bear.
He dreams of cookies, warm and sweet,
While tripping over his own two feet!

A family feast, oh what a spread,
With thoughts of diet - they're all dead.
Laughter echoes, hearts are light,
In this chaos, feels just right!

Spiced Comfort

Cinnamon rolls on the counter rise,
With icing like clouds in sweet surprise.
The kids sneak bites when no one sees,
Leaving crumbs like Little Miss Muffet's peas!

Gingerbread men with eyes of gum,
Dance in the oven, oh so numb.
We ask if they can hold a tune,
They just giggle, baked in June!

Nutmeg whispers from the shelf,
Saying, 'Don't forget, treat yourself!'
But then the dog thought he'd partake,
A spiced comfort gone awry, what a mistake!

Baking chaos? It's just routine,
With flour footprints, a cotton candy scene.
But in this mess, we find our bliss,
In spiced comfort, can't resist!

Luminescent Treats

Cookies glowing like stars at night,
With sprinkles shining, oh what a sight!
The batter's so bright, it could spark,
A culinary rave in our backyard park!

Brownies glitter with a sugary sheen,
The ultimate treat, you know what I mean?
But watch out, Mom says, 'Not too much!'
As we dive in like it's a magic punch!

Chocolate rivers star in our dreams,
With marshmallow clouds, bursting at the seams.
Our sweet tooth grows to monstrous height,
As we bake through the day and into the night!

In the end, it's all about cheer,
With luminescent treats, we huddle here.
The giggles and joy, they can't be beat,
Together we savor every sweet!

Cinnamon-Crafted Comforts

Whisking dreams in a frothy bowl,
As cinnamon curls around the soul.
Pies cooling on windows, oh what bliss,
Who knew baking was like a magic kiss?

Cookies in shape of a pet cat,
Mom says, 'No more eating, or a spat!'
But as the dough's too tempting to resist,
We sneak a bite and then assist!

The scent of warmth, a hug from the oven,
A comfort found in the happiness woven.
Even a spill can't lead to gloom,
We'll just add sprinkles and boom, boom, boom!

So here's to the mess we'll call home,
In cinnamon-crafted, we'll gladly roam.
Laughter and love wrap around tight,
As we bake our world, oh what a delight!

Whispers of Sweet Spice

In the pantry, spices talk,
Ginger and cinnamon, they squawk.
Nutmeg winks, paprika grins,
Nutty banter as the baking begins.

Flour dust dances, light and bright,
Sugar sneezes, what a sight!
The mixer hums a silly song,
As merry ingredients all get along.

Butter whispers, 'Let's get creamed,'
Eggs chuckle, 'We're a great team!'
Sifting joy, laughter's the glue,
Baking's a party, just for you!

A pie erupts, "Look at my crust!"
The brownies chirp, "In us, you trust!"
Desserts unite, a sweet parade,
In this kitchen, fun's always made.

Hearthside Haven

By the hearth, cozy chairs sit,
Blankets piled, a perfect fit.
A cat naps while the fire crackles,
Dreaming of fish and other shackles.

Grandpa's stories, oh what a hoot,
Uncle Bob's jokes? They're quite a fluke!
S'mores ready, chocolate drips,
With marshmallows, we share our quips.

The dog snorts with time to spare,
Chasing shadows through the air.
As laughter echoes, good vibes swell,
This hearthside haven, where all is well.

With mugs of cocoa, we make a toast,
To silly moments that we love the most.
So gather 'round, let the laughter flow,
In this warm hug, let the memories grow.

Sugar Spun Architecture

With candy canes and gumdrop bricks,
We build our dreams with sweet tooth tricks.
A licorice roof, so splendid and neat,
Gumdrops for windows, a sugary treat.

The frosting flows like a creamy stream,
"Watch for the roof!" gives a sugar scream.
Candy arches, delicate and fair,
Tilting precariously in the sweet air.

A marshmallow pond, frothy and bright,
Where jelly bean fish swim with delight.
This edible town, oh what a sight,
Built by giggles, love at first bite.

But oh dear! A sneeze threatens doom,
Our masterpiece risks a sugary tomb!
With a laugh and a cheer, we rebuild it again,
In sugar-spun bliss, we'll always win!

Flickering Warmth

The candle flickers, shadows dance,
Whispers of glow, a merry prance.
A toast to mischief, cheeky and bright,
As shadows wiggle in the soft light.

The cookies burn, oops, what a mess!
With smoke alarms singing, we feel the stress.
But laughter erupts, who cares about treats?
Our hearts are filled with the greatest feats!

A fireplace crackles, wood pops and sings,
As fun flies in on invisible wings.
We tickle the bellies, share some cheer,
With warmth and joy, our friends are near.

So here's to the flicker, for laughter we chase,
In moments like these, we find our place.
Through giggles and warmth, let's hold on tight,
In the flickering glow, our spirits ignite!

Fireside Fairytales

Once a dragon sought to bake,
In a kitchen, for goodness sake.
He mixed the dough with fright,
Made cookies that took flight!

The gingerbread men ran away,
Yelling 'Not today, hooray!'
The dragon cried, 'What a mess!'
He now burns his snacks, no less!

A knight came in with a grin,
Asked for cakes, he was all in.
But the dragon's oven roared,
And the knight was left ignored!

So now we tell, by the fire's glow,
Of dragons who can't bake, oh no!
Let them roast marshmallows instead,
For pastries leave them filled with dread!

Warming Whispers

A bear with a tea set, how quaint,
Brewing gossip that's far from faint.
He spills the tea with ease,
As rabbits quiver and squeeze!

Sipping slowly, he starts to snore,
The teapot clinks upon the floor.
The mice plot to steal his brew,
But the bear wakes up with a 'Boo!'

A wise old owl joins the fun,
He thinks it's all a clever run.
'Why sip alone when friends are near?'
So they all joined, and shout with cheer!

Now they whisper tales so grand,
In a cozy, laughter-filled land.
With scones and jam beside the fire,
Their friendship grows ever higher!

The Comfort of Confections

In a land where chocolates rain,
A squirrel sat munching in vain.
He claimed every piece in sight,
Then slipped, oh what a plight!

Cakes were piled up high like a tower,
He thought himself quite the flower.
But frosting slipped, and what a sound!
Chocolate avalanche all around!

His friends all laughed at his sticky state,
'Next time, buddy, just don't overrate!'
But he shrugged with a sugary smile,
'I'll just glide through this mess for a while!'

So they feasted on sweets, joyous and bright,
A confectionery dream in pure delight.
And from that day, they all would say,
'Indulging is fine if you play!'

Edible Abodes

There once was a house made of pie,
With a crust that reached for the sky.
But ants sought to claim,
The front porch, just lame!

A donut sat on the roof,
Proclaiming, 'I'm sweet, that's the truth!'
While chocolate bars stacked so high,
Whispered, 'We surely won't die!'

Then one day a hungry dear,
Came munching and left us in fear.
'This could be our last, ohhh!'
The pie said, 'Let's go slow!'

But with a giggle and crunch of delight,
The animals gathered for a bite.
In this edible home, full of cheer,
They feasted together without any fear!

Cozy Whims of Winter Tales

In blankets thick where snowflakes dance,
We sip hot cocoa, take a chance.
The cat in socks, a fuzzy sight,
Pretends to guard the warmth tonight.

Outside the window, icebergs form,
While we are safe and snug from harm.
The snowman wears my scarf anew,
And I just hope he doesn't snooze!

The fire crackles with a cheer,
While my dog dreams of chasing deer.
A marshmallow plops, oh what a splash,
Turned into cocoa, oh what a crash!

So here we sit, with tales to spin,
Of winter's charm and belly grins.
With laughter loud, through snow we'll roam,
In our cozy whimsy of winter's home.

Frosty Fragrances and Flickering Glow

The candles flicker, scents collide,
A mix of pine and ginger glide.
The cookies burn, oh what a sin,
But still, I'll munch and wear that grin.

Hot cider warms my chilly hands,
While snowballs fly like merry bands.
My cat jumped high to chase a frog,
But landed right in a snowy bog!

The Christmas lights now twinkle bright,
But tangled up, they caused a fright.
I swear this year I'll sort them right,
But first, let's laugh by candlelight!

So here's to frost and mischief's art,
To cozy cheer and merry heart.
As winter plays its playful show,
We bask in frosty scents aglow.

Candy Lane Dreams

In the land of sweets, where dreams reside,
Candy canes grow on the roadside.
Chocolate rivers flow with glee,
I think I'll swim—just wait for me!

The gumdrop trees sway in the breeze,
Whispering sweet nothings with ease.
A licorice fox, oh what a sight,
Chasing marshmallows under moonlight!

Fudge frosting covers the ground so brown,
Oh, what joy in this sugar town.
Frosting fights break out with a grin,
But we all hug tight and laugh within.

So let's indulge in this candied place,
Where every treat has a teasing face.
In Candy Lane, we'll never tire,
For sugary dreams spark our heart's fire.

Ember-lit Euphoria

As embers dance, they crack and pop,
A cozy seat, I won't switch, stop!
S'mores all melt while stories fly,
And laughter rises to the sky.

The socks on my feet mismatched today,
But cozy warmth is here to stay.
A sweater hug from head to toe,
In ember light, my heart's aglow.

Hot dogs roast and there's a schmooze,
Though I forgot to bring my booze.
The joy of friends, that's the best part,
Under the stars, we share our heart.

With flickering flames and tales we weave,
Late into night, we choose to believe.
Ember-lit happiness shines so bright,
In this euphoria of warm delight.

Sweet Hearths and Sugar Dreams

In the kitchen, cookies bake,
The cat's sneaking bites, for heaven's sake!
Flour on his nose, what a sight,
Sweet dreams arise in the soft moonlight.

Marshmallow clouds float on hot cocoa seas,
Laughter erupts like the buzzing bees.
Grandma's secrets spill from her lips,
While chocolate's melting in gooey drips.

Sugar sprinkles dance, joyfully swirl,
The mixer's going wild, watch it twirl!
With every mishap, we share a wide grin,
Sweet hearths and sugar dreams, let the fun begin!

Flickers in the Frost

Snowflakes tumble, a soft ballet,
While the dog prances, hatching a play.
I slip and slide on ice like a fool,
Creating new moves, a wintertime school.

Breath turns to clouds, a frosty puff,
We build a snowman, though it's rather rough.
He's got a top hat, but it's on his knee,
Flickers of laughter under the tree.

Hot tea in hand, we whisper and cheer,
As penguins invade our frosty frontier.
With mittens mismatched, and noses red,
Flickers in the frost, let the fun spread!

Spiced Shadows Beneath the Eaves

Gingerbread men run from the oven's roar,
A gathered crowd just wants one more!
Whiskers twitch as the spices blend,
From heaven above, sweet scents descend.

The shadows dance as the candles flick,
While elves are hiding, think they're slick.
With mischief abound, they take a peek,
Spiced shadows yawn, the night's not bleak.

Pinecones chatter, gossiping trees,
Secrets exchanged with the winter breeze.
A cozy quilt wraps around the glee,
Spiced shadows beneath, how merry we be!

Whispers in the Winter Glow

The fire crackles, a warm embrace,
As tales of penguins fill the space.
Snowmen argue over hats and scarves,
Whispers in the winter glow, how it starves!

Pajamas are loud, a fashion faux pas,
We laugh at each other, it's quite the bazaar.
Hot cocoa spills, a little delight,
With marshmallows bobbing like ships in the night.

The wind sings a tune, a frosty affair,
While dad wears a scarf like he hasn't a care.
We snuggle together, much joy to bestow,
Whispers in the winter glow, let it flow!

Crumbs of Candlelight

In the kitchen, crumbs take flight,
As I bake a cake by candlelight.
Flour flies, and eggs do crack,
Sugar sprinkles, but where's the snack?

The frosting's thick, a mountain high,
I dip my finger, oh me, oh my!
But wait, what's this? A sneaky cat,
Tasting my treat – how rude is that?

The candles flicker, shadows sway,
The dog joins in, hip-hip-hooray!
Baking's fun, till things go wrong,
Now the fire alarm sings its song!

With flour on my nose and joy in heart,
I'll be a baker, a true sweet arts!
But for now, let's eat the crumbs,
Before the smoke alarm goes, "Drums!"

Cozy Confections and Ember Tales

In a cozy nook with treats aplenty,
I sip my cocoa, oh so gently.
Marshmallows floating like little dreams,
Stirring up laughter and silly schemes.

Chocolate bars stacked to the sky,
Every bite makes the taste buds sigh.
But then, a sneeze! Oh, what a mess,
Cocoa explosion – I must confess!

Candies giggle in the night,
While gumdrops shimmer in the light.
A cookie jumps, oh what a sight,
It wobbles away, escaping the bite!

Cozy vibes and tasty tales,
With every munch, the joy prevails.
So let's indulge 'til the stars turn bright,
In this sweet world, all feels just right.

Frosted Fantasies by Flickering Flames

Frosted cupcakes in a line,
Sparkling sprinkles, oh divine!
But one rolls off, and what a mess,
It lands right on my favorite dress!

The flames crackle, shadows dance,
My baking skills? A daring chance!
With every whisk and beat of cream,
I wonder if this is a baking dream.

Candles drip like a sweetened rain,
I try to wipe but cause more pain.
The dog steals a treat, oh what a show,
Now I'm the one left saying "No!"

Yet in the chaos, joy is found,
Laughter echoes, a joyful sound.
So here's to sweets, both big and small,
In this frosted fantasy, we love them all!

Sugarplum Sanctuaries

In a land of sugarplums so bright,
Candy canes and cookies in sight.
A gingerbread house, can't resist,
But wait, is that icing on my fist?

Marzipan creatures prance around,
While chocolate rivers flow, profound.
I take a dip; oh what a crave,
Now I'm sticky, like a sugar wave!

Fairy lights twinkle, oh so fairy,
But watch your step, the floor is scary.
A marshmallow pit? Oh, what a treat,
Till I'm stuck, and can't use my feet!

In this sanctuary, let's dance and glide,
With giggles and sweets for every ride.
So join the fun, we'll laugh till dawn,
In this sugarplum haven, we'll carry on!

Radiance and Recipe

In the kitchen, sparks do fly,
Mixing flour with a pinch of pie.
The eggs dance in a bowl so wide,
While sugar whispers, "Come, let's ride!"

A sprinkle here, a dash of fun,
Baking's a race, but I can't run.
I pull a cake out, it's quite a show,
With frosting glimmers, all aglow!

My friends all say, "What a delight!"
But I'm just glad it didn't take flight.
We take a bite, and oh what bliss,
But who knew cake could be like this?

So here's the joke upon the plate,
Our laughter's the best ingredient fate.
With each warm bite, our chuckles rise,
In the kitchen, joy never dies!

A Palette of Frosting

Colors swirl, it's quite a sight,
Frosting fights with a spatula's bite.
Pink and green, a rainbow's tease,
My cake's a canvas, put me at ease!

I squeeze and squiggle, a sweet parade,
But somehow, I've made a lemon charade.
The purple's a flop, the blue's too thin,
My masterpiece cries, "Let the chaos begin!"

With candies and sprinkles set aside,
A lollipop soldier joins the ride.
As friends all gather, we sway and sing,
With frosting on faces, what joy we bring!

So grab your fork, don't be a bore,
A slice of this cake will leave you wanting more!
Through giggles and crumbs, we slather it right,
For in our laughter, the frosting shines bright!

Warm Embraces

Oh, the hugs that come from doughy hands,
Kneaded and shaped like life's best plans.
A doughy ball rolls, it won't sit still,
My cuddly kitchen, such warmth, what thrill!

From floury hugs to cinnamon flares,
Each warm embrace is a treat that shares.
Cookies baking make the house manic,
Leaving sweet scents that feel quite organic!

Friends come over, a floury crew,
Smiles and laughter as we all chew.
With cookie crumbs dancing on our cheek,
Every hug shared is the joy we seek!

Let's raise a toast to doughy delight,
As we mix up love in this kitchen tonight.
With every bite, the warmth we chase,
A recipe crafted of warm embraces!

Baked Wishes Under Stars

Under the stars, we dream up our fate,
Baking wishes on plates that can wait.
With dough in hand, we toss it around,
And sprinkle hopes on the ground!

What's a wish without a sweet taste?
A cookie for thoughts that can't go to waste.
We giggle and sigh as we shape each grin,
A cupcake for hopes where dreams begin!

The oven hums a lullaby slow,
As warmth wraps us in its gentle glow.
Our wishes rise like the dough in the pan,
Under the twinkling stars, we make our plan!

So share a slice, and don't let it cool,
For laughter's the secret, our precious jewel.
With baked wishes whispered and dreams sincere,
Let's eat up the stars, we're all pioneers!

Aesthetic Abodes

In a house made of cheese, I dream and I dwell,
With walls made of crackers, oh what a swell!
My fridge is a fountain, with soda on tap,
Each room holds adventures, like a crazy map.

The bathroom's a sauna, with chocolate mousse,
The toilet sings ballads, oh what a truce!
My sofa's a cloud, it floats way up high,
On weekends, we watch candy rain from the sky.

A closet of socks, they do tango and sway,
While the lamp taps its foot, keeping blues at bay.
Each corner has giggles, with pillows that tease,
In this house of pure whimsy, I'm always at ease.

With gardens of jellybeans, vibrant and bright,
Sunsets of cupcake, oh what a sight!
I invite all my friends for a party of cheer,
In my aesthetic abode, where laughter's the sphere.

Sweets and Stories

Cookies whisper secrets beneath sugar's glaze,
While marshmallows dance in a caramel haze.
Every pie tells a tale of a baking spree,
In a world made of sweets, come share it with me.

Chocolate rivers flow, with fudge waterfalls,
Gummy bears gossip in candy-floss halls.
Donuts have stories, in sprinkles they dress,
Sharing joys and sorrows, oh what a mess!

Cupcake houses sway, with frosting so thick,
Each flavor a saga, some sweet, some quite sick.
Lollipops laugh loudly, in hues bright and bold,
Their tales of adventure are better than gold.

Come savor the laughter, the frosting so fun,
In a land of delights that's never undone.
With each sugary bite, a new tale unfolds,
In the land of sweet stories, where happiness molds.

Honeyed Harmonies

In a garden of bees, they hum a sweet song,
Dancing on petals, where flowers belong.
Honey drips down from the sky like a dream,
Life's sweeter with bees buzzin' round in a team.

A bear with a banjo, strumming in glee,
Plays tunes to the trees, oh, listen with me!
The flowers all sway as the melody swirls,
In harmony, hummingbirds dart and twirl.

The sunbeams join in with their golden delight,
While ladybugs tap dance, all day and night.
They gather their nectar, their voices unite,
In a chorus of friendship, everything's right.

So grab a sweet jar, let the music ascend,
Join the buzzing brigade, where fun has no end.
In honeyed harmonies, find joy that won't fade,
With every sweet note, a bright memory made.

Nutmeg Nostalgia

In the kitchen, cinnamon whispers hello,
Nutmeg's a wizard, casting spices in flow.
Remember the cookies that Mom used to bake?
Each bite brought a smile, oh, what a great shake!

Grandma's tales brewed like a warm cup of tea,
Of gingerbread houses beneath sugar trees.
As nutmeg swirls in, memories ignite,
In this fragrant embrace, everything feels right.

Pumpkin pies sing with their crusts all aglow,
While memories simmer, like a sweet, gentle flow.
The laughter and warmth fill the air like a song,
In the heart of our kitchen, where we all belong.

So whip up some laughter in bowls, big and round,
With nutmeg nostalgia, sweet memories abound.
Each sprinkle of joy, a taste from the past,
In this gathering of love, may the moments last.

Milton Keynes UK
Ingram Content Group UK Ltd.
UKHW022122091224
452185UK00010B/463